Contents

What is a map?

A map is a drawing of the real world, or part of it, on a piece of paper or an electronic screen, such as a computer. Over 4,000 years ago, Babylonians in the Middle East carved the first maps on clay slabs. Other early maps were drawn on cloth, so the word map comes from the Latin word "mappa", meaning cloth or sheet.

This street map illustrates how you can see a much larger area from above than from the ground.

MAPS TODAY
Nowadays, almost any kind of data can be fed into a computer, displayed on an electronic map in relation to other data, and updated as changes occur. There are maps to show almost anything.

A BIRD'S EYE VIEW
A map is often a view of the Earth looking down from above, like a bird looking down from the sky. This makes it easier to see where things are and how they relate to other things.

LOOKING AT
MAPS

Barbara Taylor

W
FRANKLIN WATTS

First published in 2007 by

Franklin Watts

338 Euston Road

London NW1 3BH

Franklin Watts Australia

Hachette Children's Books

Level 17/207 Kent Street

Sydney NSW 2000

Editor: Jeremy Smith

Consultant: Steve Watts

(FRGS, Principal Lecturer University of Sunderland)

Art director: Jonathan Hair

Design: Mo Choy

Artwork: John Alston

Picture researcher: Kathy Lockley

Acknowledgements:

AA World Travel Library 12. Aflo Photo Agency/Alamy Images 3b, 23, COVER. AIAT
Monte Rosa Walser, Villa Deslex, I-11025 Gressoney-Saint-Jean (AO), 16. Colin
Cuthbert/Science Photo Library 32. Dartmouth Flood Observatory – 2005 Flood Archive
8. Jon Davidson/Lonely Planet Images 7. Mark Gibson/Alamy Images 21. Robert Harding
Picture Library 37. Justin Kase/Alamy Images 20. Will & Deni McIntyre/Science Photo
Library 24. ©1996 MAGELLAN Geographix, Santa Barbara, CA/Corbis 13. Steven
May/Alamy Images 27. NASA 34/5. NASA/Goddard Space Flight Center Image by Reto
Stockli/The Visible Earth: 38T. NASA/JPL 9. NOAA/Dept of Commerce 11. Polar
Adventures Ltd 40. Philippe Psaila/Science Photo Library 43. Public Records
Office/Heritage-Images Partnership 19. Rex Features 14. Tom Van Sant/Geosphere
Project, Santa Monica/Science Photo Library 17. Franklin Watts 22, 38b.

A CIP catalogue record for this book
is available from the British Library.

ISBN 10: 0 7496 6779 6

ISBN 13: 9 7807 4966 7795

Dewey Classification 912'.014

Printed in China

Franklin Watts is a division of Hachette Children's Books.

MAPS AND THE REAL WORLD

To help you understand how maps are different from the real world, try drawing your own map of your classroom, your bedroom or any other room around your house.

First take a photograph of the place you have chosen, while standing on the ground. Then, take a photograph looking down on the place from a high point, such as a staircase or a stepladder. (Ask an adult to help you with a stepladder.)

Now use the photographs to help you draw a sketch map looking straight down on the place from above. Make sure all the objects are in the right place in relation to each other but don't worry about exact sizes and positions for now.

Can you think of different ways to use your map? It might help you to re-design rooms or open spaces.

Maps help people to find their way around in built-up cities such as New York (where high buildings block the line of sight).

KEY SKILLS

Throughout this book, you will learn different skills. Each different skill is represented by one of the following icons:

 Completing a practical activity

 Analysing information

 Working with graphs, maps, diagrams and photographs

 Looking at global issues

 Researching information

 Observing

How are maps used?

People use different maps for different purposes. When people move house, visit relatives, or go on holiday, maps help them to find their way around new places. Geographers use maps to: locate things, show relationships, prove ideas and ask questions.

WHO USES MAPS?

Geographers use maps to prepare reports about things such as traffic patterns and migration of people. Town planners use maps to assess the impact of new buildings, such as supermarkets or shopping centres, on the local environment. Journalists use maps to illustrate newspaper reports while archaeologists and historians use maps to study ancient cultures.

WARNING SIGNS

Geologists use maps to plan where to drill for oil or construct roads or new buildings. They can also use them to work out where disasters such as earthquakes and volcanic eruptions are most likely to occur.

A map showing the areas most at risk of flooding (marked orange) is a useful tool for geographers, environmentalists and other people.

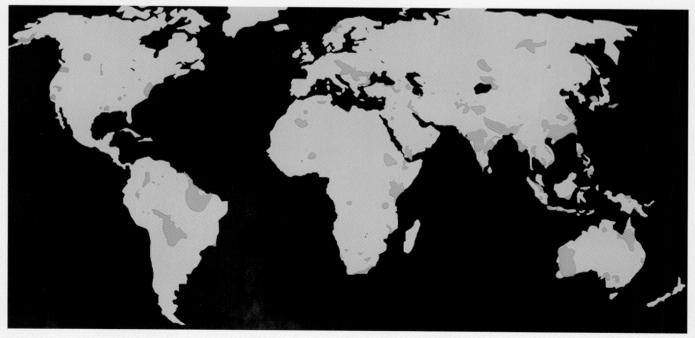

This view of Venus' landscape was generated by data collected from space by the Magellan probe.

OUT OF THIS WORLD

Maps are not just useful here on Earth. Maps of the Moon or other planets help scientists to learn more about the Solar System. They also help scientists plan where to land probes or spacecraft and to discover which planets might be most suited for settlements out in space one day.

WHICH MAP TO USE?

See if you can make a list of all the different kinds of maps you can think of. Your list might include: road maps, relief maps, weather maps, tourist maps and world maps. Now think carefully about the situations described in the list on the right. Which sort of map would be most useful in each situation? You may need more than one kind of map in some situations.

HELPING HAND

Look on the Internet and in libraries, newspapers, tourist information centres, travel agents, museums, galleries, train stations, atlases and nature reserves to find different kinds of map.

CHOOSE A MAP FOR:

- A train journey from one town to another.
- A skiing trip.
- A news report on a war zone.
- A study of river pollution.
- A report showing where to draw the borders of a national park.
- A trip to a shopping centre.
- A survey of traffic flow in a town.
- Where to ride a bike through a forest.
- Where to build new homes near a river.
- A teacher giving a history lesson about explorers.

Scale

A landscape map shows features such as hills, valleys, rivers, coasts, roads, towns and cities. It is impossible to show things the same size as they are in real life, so everything is shrunk down by the same amount to fit. This is called drawing to scale. Not all types of map are drawn to scale.

This small-scale map covers a large area. It shows main roads, and main settlements.

This larger-scale map shows an area of the same landscape in much more detail.

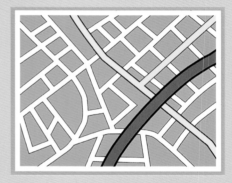

At an even larger scale you can see every street in this part of the landscape.

MAP SCALES

The scale on a landscape map tells you how the size of things in real life compares with the size that they appear on the map. You can use a map scale to work out the actual size, height and dimensions of the features on the map. Maps can be drawn to any scale, but some scales are used more than others. The scale is usually written as a ratio, such as 1:25,000. This means that one unit of measurement on the map represents 25,000 of the same units in real life.

LARGE SCALE, SMALL SCALE

Very large-scale maps cover a small area of land in great detail. They may even show individual buildings. Small-scale maps cover large areas of land with little detail. They are ideal for travelling long distances by car or train.

Maps often have a linear scale. In this example, one centimetre equals 100 metres in real life.

	100	200	300	400	500	600	700	800	900	1km

SCALE GUIDE
1: 10,000 (1cm = 10,000cm or 10cm = 1km)
– useful for maps with street details for town planners
1: 25,000 (1cm = 25,000cm or 4cm = 1km)
– useful for walkers and outdoor activities
1: 50,000 (1cm = 50,000cm or 2cm = 1km)
– useful for short journeys or planning a day out
1: 125,000 (1cm = 125,000cm or 1cm = 1.25km)
– useful for drivers going on long journeys

This electronic map of the USA is based on real data collected by NASA. It is possible to zoom in and look at individual states in details.

On an electronic map, the scale is less important as you can zoom in and out and view the map at lots of different scales. The original data is still captured at a particular scale though.

MAKING SCALE MAPS
On an A4 piece of paper, draw a square 20cm by 20cm. Divide up the square into a hundred 2cm squares. On top of the squares, draw an outline picture of one or two objects, such as an animal or a car.

On another piece of paper, draw a square 10cm by 10cm. Divide up this square into 1cm squares. Then copy your picture onto this smaller square, making sure that the same lines appear in the same squares. You will end up with a 1:2 scale drawing. The smaller drawing is half the size of the big one. All the distances are half the length of those on the big drawing.

HELPING HAND
Another way of writing a scale is to use a bar divided into units, like the one on page 10. Each unit represents the same distance. This is called a linear scale. See www.junglephotos.com/galapagos/gmaps/aboutmaps/scale.shtml for another example of linear scale.

ALBERS EQUAL AREA PROJECTION
MOSAIC OF FIFTEEN AVHRR IMAGES
24 MAY, 1984 - 14 MAY, 1986

Distance

The scale on a landscape map is used to convert the distance between two points into the distance in real life. This gives people an idea of how long their journeys will take. String or wool can be used to measure distances very accurately because it can measure curved lines. Straight-line distances on a map can be measured using a ruler – this is sometimes called "as the crow flies". It is useful over long distances, but not as accurate.

KEY SKILLS

Gathering data

Working with maps

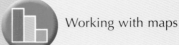

Analysing evidence and drawing conclusions; interpreting maps; explaining geographical features

HELPING HAND
Look back at pages 10–11 to remind yourself about map scales and how they work.

HOW LONG IS A PIECE OF STRING?

Use a piece of string or wool to trace the route between two places, making sure you follow all the twists and turns in the roads or paths.

Mark the string or wool at the beginning and end of the route. Then measure the total length of the route on a ruler or a tape measure.

Use the scale on the map to convert the distance on the map into the distance in the real place.

This man is using a piece of string to work out the quickest route between two places in the Yorkshire Dales, England.

WHAT IS THE DISTANCE?

Choose a small-scale map of a large area or a whole country and work out accurate distances between ten of the large towns or cities. You could choose a large-scale map and work out the distance between four separate points. People do this to calculate how long it will take them to get there.

If the route is in straight lines, you could use a ruler for the measurement. For curved lines you could use string, wool or a piece of paper. To use a piece of paper for measuring distance, first place a corner of the straight edge of the paper at your starting point. Follow the route and every time it curves away from the straight edge of the paper, make a mark. Turn the paper until the edge is on the route again.

Keep doing this until you reach the end of your route. You should end up with a line of marks along the edge of the paper. Now measure the total distance along the edge of the paper with a ruler and use the scale to convert this measurement into the real distance.

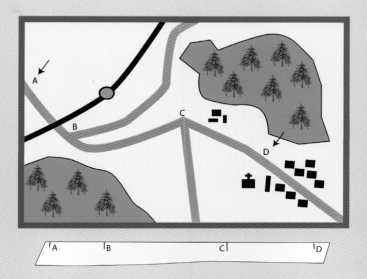

Use this map of the Santa Fe National Historic Trail to work out the distances between key places on the route. The scale is marked on the bottom of the map in miles.

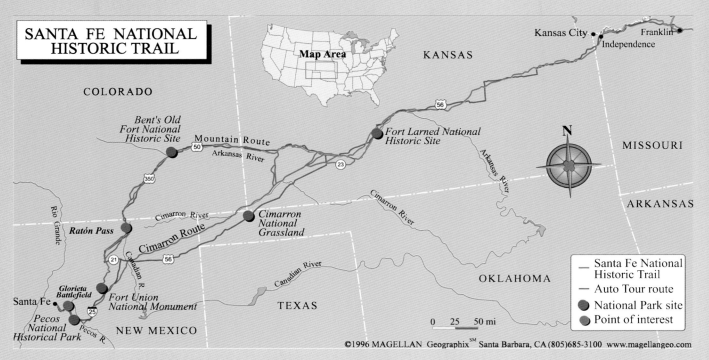

©1996 MAGELLAN Geographix℠ Santa Barbara, CA (805)685-3100 www.magellangeo.com

13

Grids

A map grid is a network of lines drawn over a map, which divides the map into squares. The ends of the lines have letters or numbers so that every square or point on the map has its own unique set of numbers or letters, which is called a grid reference.

GRID REFERENCES

Grid references help people to find places on maps quickly, easily and accurately. Different countries use different types of grids on their maps, but a map usually has instructions on how to use its own grid. A grid reference refers to a square on a map. It gives the numbers or letters for the two lines that cross each other in the bottom left-hand corner of the square.

Three soldiers are using grid references on this map to find out where they need to get to on their training mission.

READING AND MARKING GRID REFERENCES

Grid references can be given as four- or six-point numbers. First you read the numbers along the bottom or top of the map (the horizontal reference), then those along the side (the vertical reference). Six-point references are more precise than four-point references, which only point to the bottom left corner of the grid square. To write a six-point reference, locate your point within the grid square. Then, in your head, divide the square up into ten parts (along the bottom and side, from one to ten). Add these numbers to the 4-point horizontal and vertical reference respectively.

HELPING HAND
Look at pages 36 and 37 to find out how a grid of lines called latitude and longitude lines helps people to find places on world maps.

A four-point grid reference
The reference for Brook Farm is: 15 56

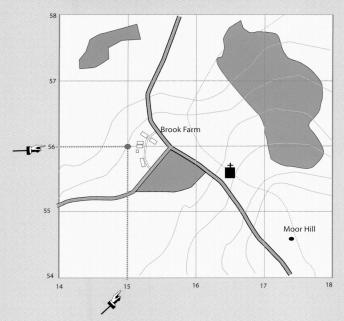

A six-point grid reference
The reference for the church is: 164 556

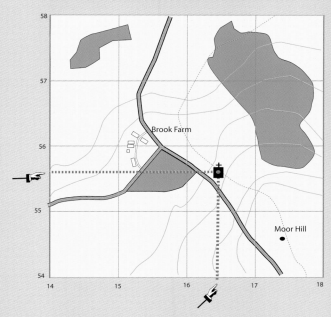

BE A TOUR GUIDE

Imagine you are a tour guide on a large holiday island. You have been asked to draw a map giving people directions to the various places of interest on the island.

First, draw a sketch map of your ideal holiday island. Your map will not be drawn to scale, so you can include large pictures of the different features, such as beaches, coral reefs, adventure parks, swimming pools, a water sports centre, a wildlife reserve, mountain temples, ski slopes, hotels and camp sites.

Draw a grid of equal-sized squares over your island and then number the ends of the grid lines. Work out grid references for each place of interest and list these underneath your map.

Write a story about the island using the grid references instead of the names of the places.

Height

The real world is not flat and map makers have different ways of showing the height and shape of the land. Some maps have raised surfaces, but they cannot be printed in books or folded up easily. Computers can produce very realistic landscapes and even turn them around so you can see them from different heights and angles. Flat maps cannot do this, however, and rely on other techniques.

A map of central Italy showing spot heights, contour lines and colour shading to indicate height to the reader.

SHOWING HEIGHT

On a flat map, artists illustrate the ups and downs on the land by using colour shading, spot heights, or contour lines, which join places that are at the same height. Hills and mountains may be shown on maps with shading, which makes high land stand out from the lower land around it. Lines called hachures get thicker as the land gets steeper. Spot heights show the exact height at a particular point on the map.

RELIEF MAPS

The geographical word for the height and shape of the land is "relief". Colour can be used to show relief on maps. The very highest points are usually shown in white.

16

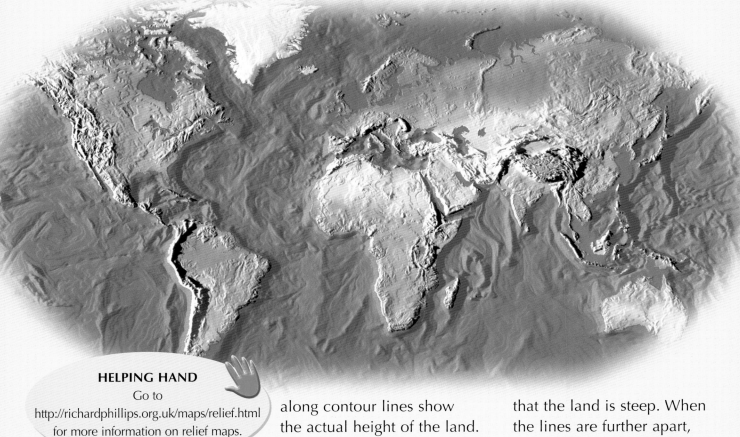

A relief map of the world. The raised areas show the most mountainous regions.

HELPING HAND
Go to
http://richardphillips.org.uk/maps/relief.html
for more information on relief maps.

CONTOUR LINES

The clearest way of showing height on a map is with thin brown lines called contour lines. The numbers written along contour lines show the actual height of the land. The lines usually increase at regular intervals, such as twenty metres. Contour lines join points of equal height. The lines never cross. When contour lines are close together, they show that the land is steep. When the lines are further apart, they indicate flatter land.

Look at maps of your local area and see if you can find patterns similar to those shown here. Once you learn to recognise these patterns, it will help you to imagine the landscape and bring a map to life.

Two maps showing height using contours. The one on the far left is a low-lying area, while the nearest map shows areas of steeper ground.

Symbols

Landscape maps use symbols instead of words to stand for real-life features, which can be physical features (such as rivers) or human features (such as railway lines). Symbols can be small pictures, letters, lines or coloured areas, which remind people of the features they represent. Most maps have a list to explain what the different symbols stand for. This list is called a key or legend. It allows people to read the language of the map.

Recycling

Telephone

Camping

Picnic Area

SIMPLE SYMBOLS

Map symbols allow a lot of information to fit into a small space. Some symbols are simple versions of the real thing, such as trees, rivers or roads. Other symbols show the idea of the feature, such as a mask for a theatre, a knife and fork for a restaurant or an elephant for a wildlife reserve.

Letters are sometimes used instead of symbols, such as PO for post office or H for hospital.

DESIGNING YOUR OWN MAP SYMBOLS

See if you can design your own map symbols for a map of a settlement on another planet. Draw a simple sketch map of the area – it doesn't need to be to scale – and decide on the features that you want to show. There are some design tips on the opposite page to help you get started. Keep the symbols as simple and clear as possible.

Toilets

Airport

Restaurant

Forest

Post Office

Hospital

HELPING HAND
In an atlas (a book of maps), the key is usually at the front of the book.

SYMBOL DESIGN TIPS

- Look at some real map symbols to give you ideas.
- Clear, simple shapes with a few, bold lines work best.
- Solid shapes are easier to see than outlines.

- You do not always have to show the actual shape of the feature, just give an idea of how it is used.
- Draw several different versions of each symbol and try out your ideas on your friends. See if they can guess what your symbols stand for.
- Draw a key to explain your symbols.

This map of Canada and Newfoundland shows how symbols are used to show where natural features and other resources can be found.

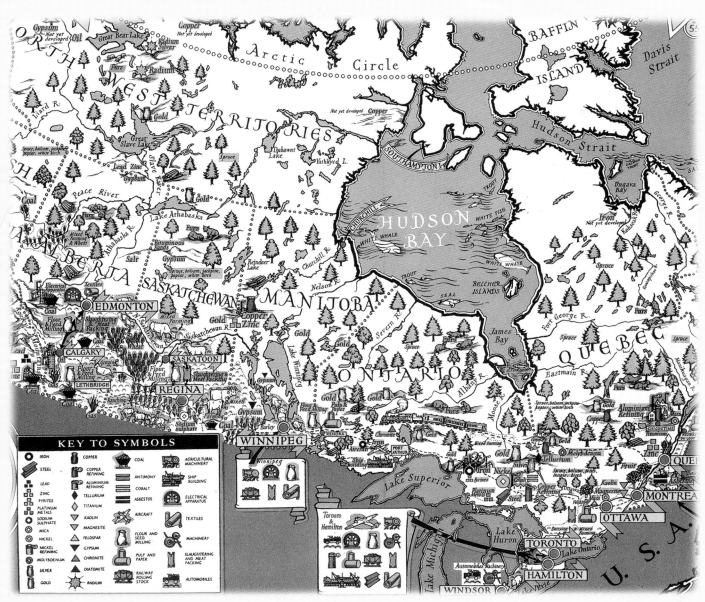

Making landscape maps

Before geographers start making a map, they have to gather as much data as possible. They walk over the land observing and measuring. They also collect information from other sources, such as interviews, surveys and photographs – from the ground or the air, from aeroplanes and satellites in space.

GLOBAL WARMING

Maps need to be constantly updated. Global warming, for example, is causing huge changes to our landscapes. Increasing levels of carbon dioxide in the atmosphere, caused by the burning of fossil fuels, prevents excess heat from escaping back into space. This causes temperatures to rise, and dries up some lakes and rivers. It has also begun to melt ice caps in the Arctic and Antarctic, causing sea levels to rise, which threatens low-lying land areas.

DRAW YOUR OWN MAP

Using the mapping skills you have learnt on pages 6–19, draw an accurate map of your playground or local park. Choose a small area that includes some distinctive features, such as play equipment, a pond, benches, fences, buildings, large trees and flower beds.

A geographer in Brittany, France takes measurements for a map using a piece of geographic sensing equipment.

Take photographs and draw a rough sketch map of the area. Then measure the size of the different features, how far apart they are and how tall they are. Use a table like the one on the opposite page to record this data, then plot the figures on your sketch map.

MAP LAYERS

A landscape map is usually made up of several different components.

1. A scale (see pages 10-11)
Geographers take accurate measurements of real things and then work out how much they need to shrink all these measurements down to fit everything on the map.

2. A grid (see pages 14-15)
A network of labelled squares over the whole map helps people find points on the map quickly and easily.

3. Symbols (see pages 18-19)
Real features on the ground are drawn as small simple shapes to save space and make the map clearer.

4. Height (see pages 16-17)
The shape of the land is represented by colours, shading, contour lines or spot heights.

HELPING HAND
The art and science of making maps is called cartography.

A cartographer checks details on a map before its publication.

SCALE

Decide how big your map is going to be and work out a scale, so that all the features will fit on a large sheet of paper. Think of a symbol for each feature and decide how you are going to show height on your map. Then draw an accurate map of your area, including a scale, a grid and a key to explain the symbols.

Feature	Size	Height	Distance from X

21

Finding the way

Maps have been used for hundreds of years to help people to find their way from one place to another. Hikers often use detailed, large-scale maps to plan and follow a route when they are walking in the countryside. To work out which direction to take, they use a compass with the map. This tells them whether to walk towards the north, south, east or west to reach their destination.

UNDERSTANDING A COMPASS

The Earth is like a giant magnet and has North and South magnetic poles, like an ordinary bar magnet. A compass has a magnetic needle, which swings around to point to the Earth's Magnetic North pole, which is slightly different from True North. Around the compass needle is a circle marked with numbers called bearings. Bearings are the most accurate way to give directions.

To help you remember the four main compass points, you could use a phrase such as: "Nobody Ever Swallows Whales". This goes from north at the top, clockwise around the compass.

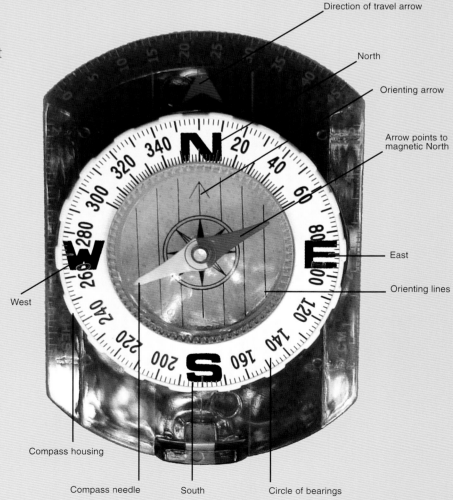

Direction of travel arrow

North

Orienting arrow

Arrow points to magnetic North

East

Orienting lines

West

Compass housing

Compass needle

South

Circle of bearings

Place the compass on the paper and make sure the direction arrow lines up with the beginning and end points of your journey.

HELPING HAND
Divide your journey into small sections, taking regular bearings to help you stay on track.

HOW TO TAKE A BEARING

1. Place your compass on the map, so that the direction of travel arrow points to your destination from where you are on the map.

2. Turn the compass housing so the orienting lines line up with the grid lines on the map. Grid north (the direction the grid lines line up with at the top of a map) is slightly different from Magnetic North. The map key will tell you how many degrees to add to your bearing to take this variation into account.

3. Hold the compass and the map horizontally, at about waist height, and turn yourself around until the compass needle swings above the orienting arrow.

4. The way the direction of travel arrow is now pointing is the bearing you need to follow to reach your destination. (Don't follow the direction of the compass needle.)

Mapping data

Ahuge variety of geographical data can be displayed in the form of a map, from human populations, diseases, life expectancy and trade to wildlife distribution, flood risk, agriculture and pollution. This kind of map links data with places, helping geographers to compare different areas easily.

KEY SKILLS

Drawing maps

Presenting information and data

Analysing evidence and drawing conclusions; interpreting maps

TYPES OF MAP

It is impossible to show all the data about a place on one map. To solve this problem, map makers have invented lots of different ways to display important data, from line maps to braille maps for the blind.

CHOROPLETH MAPS

Choropleth maps (right) use shading to show differences between areas. This map of Africa shows the difference in population density. Orange areas have the highest density, while the lightest areas are the most sparsely populated.

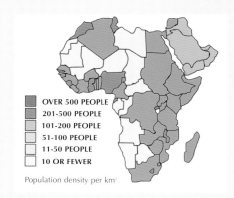

OVER 500 PEOPLE
201-500 PEOPLE
101-200 PEOPLE
51-100 PEOPLE
11-50 PEOPLE
10 OR FEWER

Population density per km²

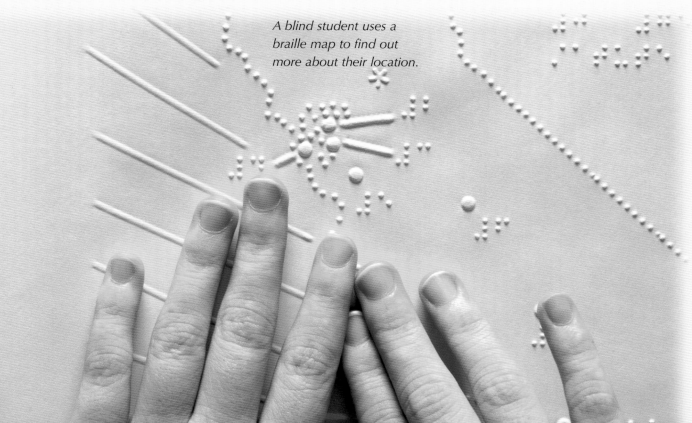

A blind student uses a braille map to find out more about their location.

TOPOLOGICAL MAPS

Topological maps (below) are maps that have been simplified to show only really important information. These maps do not usually have a scale, and distance or direction can be changed. However, the relationship beween the points remains the same. Probably the most famous example of a topological map is the London Underground map.

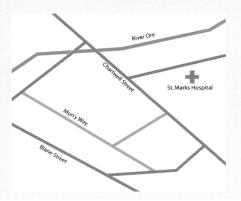

FLOW LINE MAPS

Flow line maps (below) use lines or arrows of different widths to show the value of data. Bigger numbers have wider lines or thicker arrows. The map below shows Japan's trading patterns with the rest of the world. It shows that the country trades most heavily with North America and Europe, while less trade takes place between Japan and Africa, and Japan and South America.

ISOLINE MAPS

Isoline maps (below) use lines to join points which have the same value, such as the same height (contour lines), air pressure (isobars), temperature (isotherms) or wind speed (isotachs).

The space between the isolines is shaded. The higher the value, the darker the shading. The lines on an isoline map do not cross each other.

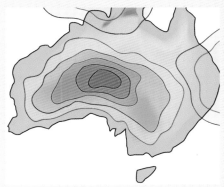

DRAW A CHOROPLETH MAP

Before you can draw a choropleth map, you will need to collect some data, such as the population in different regions of the country you live in. Make a table to record your data.

1. Divide your data into about four to eight groups, depending on the range of the numbers you have collected. Decide on a different colour for each group, using light colours to show small numbers and dark colours for high numbers. You can use different shades of the same colour if you like, since all the colours represent the same information. Draw a key to show the range of numbers each shade or colour stands for.

2. Then find or draw a map of the country divided into regions, with no other information on the map. Colour each region with the appropriate colour.

3. Stand back and look carefully at your finished map. Can you explain the distribution of the data? For instance, why do more people live in some areas than others? You may need to look at other maps, such as a landscape map, to help you answer this question.

HELPING HAND
See pages 26–27 for more about isoline maps.

Weather maps

Weather data is usually drawn as curved lines on top of a general map or a satellite image showing a particular country or part of a country. These lines mark the air movements that create the weather, and help weather forecasters to record the weather and predict how it is likely to change. Maps giving a general view of weather conditions over a large area are called synoptic charts.

HELPING HAND
Warm and cold fronts are places where warm and cold air "fight" to push each other out of the way, like a battle front in a real war.

Cold front	Occluded front	Warm front	Isobar

1032

1061

1314

called warm and cold fronts. The weather near a front is unsettled and changeable, with clouds, rain and storms.

At a warm front (shown by a line with red bumps), a mass of warm air slides up over a mass of cold air. At a cold front (shown by a line with spikes), a mass of cold air slides under a mass of warm air, pushing it upwards. An occluded front happens when a cold front merges with a warm front.

UNDERSTANDING WEATHER MAPS

The main lines on weather maps are called isobars, and they join places with the same air pressure. High air pressure usually indicates good weather, while low air pressure usually indicates bad weather. The wind blows almost parallel to the isobars. When the isobars are close together it means strong winds. When they are further apart, the winds are calmer. The boundaries between large areas of warm and cool air are marked with thicker lines

A map of the British Isles, showing weather symbols used by meteorologists.

BE A TV WEATHER FORECASTER

See if you can draw a simplified weather map, like the ones used on television weather forecasts.

First you will need to collect some weather data. Weather forecasters use data collected from weather stations, aircraft, weather satellites out in space, weather balloons and weather buoys or ships at sea. You may be able to collect data from the weather recording instruments in a Stevenson Screen or download data from a computer weather system or the Internet (for example, try www.weatherbug.com).

Prepare a sketch map of the area you are covering and draw on the isobars. Make up your own symbols for different types of weather, such as sunshine, rain, showers, cloud, wind and snow. (Look back at pages 16–17 for some tips on designing symbols.) Draw the relevant symbols on your map.

Then have a go at being a TV weather forecaster and present the weather on your map to your friends.

Moderate

Rough

Slight

Pictorial maps

Apictorial map is a special sort of map that uses large symbols or pictures to represent a theme or a particular message, such as tourist sites. Pictorial maps are often drawn by artists rather than mapmakers and are usually fun, colourful and decorative. These maps rearrange the information in order to highlight some part of it and are not usually drawn to scale.

A pictorial map of France, showing major attractions.

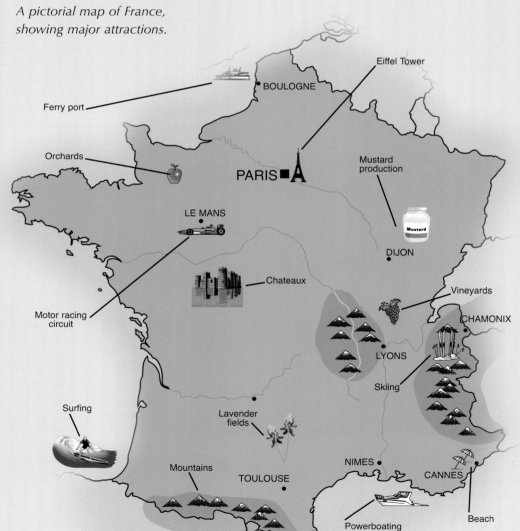

AN ARTIST'S VIEW

Pictorial maps are often humorous and include fun ways of presenting information. Tourist maps might show attractions or natural features in an amusing way. Wildlife distribution maps in animal atlases may include large pictures of the different animals. Around the edge of pictorial maps the artists may include cartoon-like strips of information and jokes. Some pictorial maps may have serious themes, such as natural disasters.

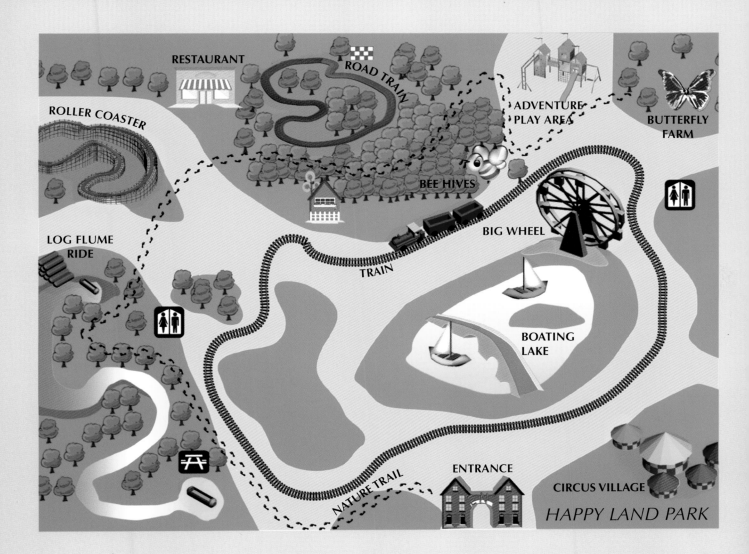

ROLLER COASTER

RESTAURANT

ROAD TRAIN

ADVENTURE PLAY AREA

BUTTERFLY FARM

BEE HIVES

LOG FLUME RIDE

BIG WHEEL

TRAIN

BOATING LAKE

ENTRANCE

NATURE TRAIL

CIRCUS VILLAGE

HAPPY LAND PARK

A THEME PARK MAP

Make up a pictorial map of your ideal theme park, showing all the rides, car parks, transport inside the park, ticket areas, restaurants and other facilities. You could paint your map, incorporate photos of a visit to a theme park or perhaps make a collage map using things such as tickets, food wrappers, cloth, shoelaces, leaves, string, wool, ridged cardboard, buttons, feathers and small pebbles (i.e. things you might collect on a visit or might represent the different rides). Think about the overall shape of the map – some pictorial maps are unusual shapes, such as the shape of a face, a castle or an animal. You don't need to draw the map to scale, just position the rides accurately in relation to each other. Make the features of the map as large as possible and draw them realistically as if you were looking at them on the ground, not looking down from above. Include a key to explain the different features and label the different sections of the theme park on the map. You could make small flags for the different sections. Around the edge of the map, see if you can draw some cartoon strips showing the following:

- The scariest rides
- The funniest rides
- The fastest rides
- The most popular rides

What is GIS?

GIS stands for Geographical Information System. It is a computer technology that is used to store, display, analyse and map information, allowing geographers to see relationships, patterns and trends. You can interact with a GIS map, using it to answer questions, visualise changes, solve problems, manage data or understand situations in the past, present and future.

KEY SKILLS

Drawing maps

Presenting and analysing data

Using ICT to communicate

Carrying out field work

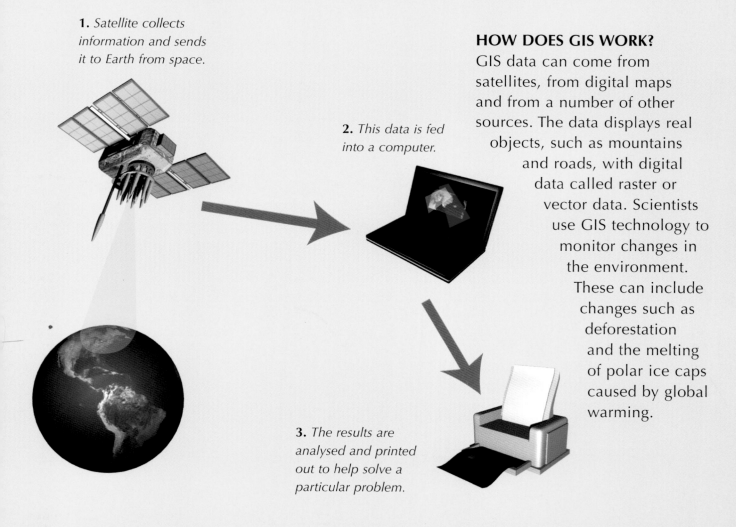

1. *Satellite collects information and sends it to Earth from space.*

2. *This data is fed into a computer.*

3. *The results are analysed and printed out to help solve a particular problem.*

HOW DOES GIS WORK?

GIS data can come from satellites, from digital maps and from a number of other sources. The data displays real objects, such as mountains and roads, with digital data called raster or vector data. Scientists use GIS technology to monitor changes in the environment. These can include changes such as deforestation and the melting of polar ice caps caused by global warming.

Halblech   **Durrach**

UPPER LAYER   *RAINFALL*

USING GIS MAPS

GIS maps are very adaptable. You can pan across a GIS map, or zoom in or out of the map, viewing it at different scales. You can point to geographic objects to find out more information about them or carry out queries and analysis.

MIDDLE LAYER   *LAND USE*

You can pull the map apart to view one or more of the layers at a time – you do not have to look at the complete map, as you do with a paper map.

BOTTOM LAYER   *EROSION (DARK RED HIGHEST LEVELS)*

You can even change a GIS map as the data changes, or change the design (such as the colour or the symbols) if you want to.

This diagram was generated using GIS data. It was used by scientists to measure and monitor erosion in two areas in Bavaria, Germany.

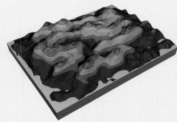

MAKING A LAYER MAP

1. Draw a map of your local town using different layers for the different types of information. Collect information about features such as car parks, shops and leisure facilities.

2. Record the data you collect onto computer tables or spreadsheets, giving each one a coded reference. Print out the data and put it into a file with a clear contents page so that people can easily find out more information about the features on your map.

3. Draw a base map of the town, showing just the main roads, buildings and open spaces. Then draw each feature on a separate layer of clear acetate. Design your own symbols to keep each layer as simple as possible. Mark the coded references to the computer data file at the relevant places on each layer.

4. Make a hole in one corner of the base map and the same corner of each layer of acetate. Tie the layers loosely together so that you can swivel one layer at a time over the base map. You can add more layers to your map in the future, or change one layer at a time, rather than having to change the whole map.

How is GIS used?

Geographical Information Systems (GIS) are most useful for answering questions and making decisions, such as where to build a new supermarket. They link information to locations, such as driving times to road networks. Unlike a paper map, they show geographers not just how things are now, but what might happen in the future if certain features of the map change.

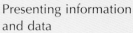

KEY SKILLS

Presenting information and data

Researching information

Asking geographical questions

Observing changes in the environment

A scientist uses a device to send the coordinates of water mains on a street map to a Geographical Information System (GIS).

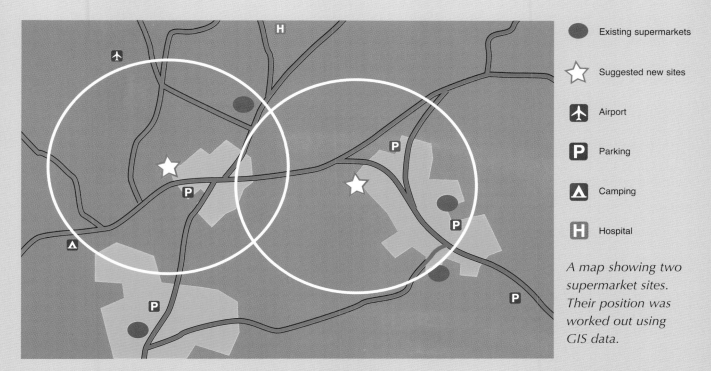

⬤	Existing supermarkets
☆	Suggested new sites
✈	Airport
P	Parking
⛺	Camping
H	Hospital

A map showing two supermarket sites. Their position was worked out using GIS data.

USING GIS MAPS

Farmers can put soil and rainfall data on top of maps of their fields to see the best places to grow crops. Data on river features, water levels and people's addresses can be combined to predict houses in danger of flooding. Maps of gas or water pipelines can be matched up with street plans to plan repairs or the replacement of pipes.

HELPING HAND

Today, most geographical information is collected in digital (number) form and fed directly into computers, but paper maps can also be converted into a series of numbers that computers "understand".

SUPERMARKET SITES

Imagine that a new supermarket chain "Fantastic Foods" wants to build a supermarket in your area. You have been asked to help them decide on the best place to build their supermarket using GIS data.

Look at a map of your local area and draw a sketch map showing the location of the existing supermarkets. Then look at the density of the housing near each supermarket and estimate how many people live within a short drive of each one. Are there enough supermarkets already, or is there room for a new one? You could carry out a survey in the town to see what the local people think.

Ask questions such as:

- How long does it take you to drive to the supermarket?
- At which supermarkets do you usually buy your food?
- Where would be the best location for a new supermarket?
- How would a new supermarket affect the local environment?

Once you have finished collecting this information, write a report for "Fantastic Foods". Include a map linking your survey results to the possible sites for their new supermarket. Choose the best site and list the main reasons for your conclusion.

Mapping change

The world around us is changing all the time. Natural changes to the landscape, such as rivers wearing away the land, often happen very slowly. There are also sudden, dramatic changes caused by events such as earthquakes or wars. Human-made changes, such as new buildings, mines or roads, also take place fairly quickly. With GIS systems and computers, it is much easier to map change and compare different maps than it is with a paper map.

KEY SKILLS

Researching information

Drawing maps

Describing and explaining geographical features; interpreting maps; analysing evidence

A satellite image of an area of Brazillian rainforest in 2001. The forest appears in red and deforested areas in blue-grey rectangles.

HELPING HAND
Look back at pages 30–33
to find out more about GIS
mapping systems.

USING MAPS

A geographer might map the paths taken by hurricanes to help predict where and when the next hurricane will take place. Comparing maps of an area before and after events such as natural disasters, for example, can help geographers plan for how to cope or prevent future catastrophes. Controllers of emergency vehicles compare maps to look for areas where lots of accidents happen.

MAPPING LOCAL CHANGE

How do you think your local area has changed over the years? Your local library or the Internet should have old photographs or maps showing what it used to look like. See if you can find some old maps of your area and compare these with some recent maps. Think about how and why the area has changed. Compare the sizes of towns and villages and the number of roads, motorways and railways. Look for farms, factories and offices and see it you can identify changes in working patterns. Are there any changes in the course of rivers or the shape of coastlines? Are there still as many forests, woodlands and open spaces as there were years ago?

You could draw a map of your local area showing all the changes that you feel would make it an ideal place in which to live. Which things would you like to keep? Which things would you like to get rid of? Think carefully about the impact your changes would have on the environment.

By 2006, the same area of Brazilian rainforest has been heavily deforested. There are about three times as many cleared areas as there were in 2001.

Latitude and longitude

On world maps, a grid of imaginary lines called longitude and latitude helps people find places on the map. Lines of longitude go from the top to the bottom of a map or a globe. Lines of latitude go across, from side to side. Longitude and latitude lines are numbered, so every place in the world can be located using the number of the latitude line first, followed by the number of the longitude line. On a world map, New York is located at 40° North (latitude) and 73° West (longitude).

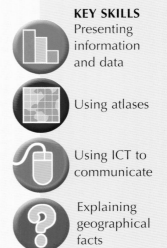

KEY SKILLS
Presenting information and data

Using atlases

Using ICT to communicate

Explaining geographical facts

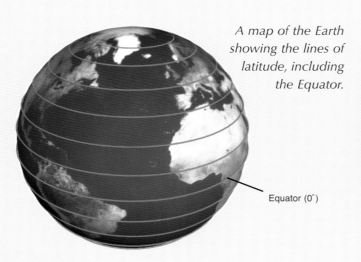

A map of the Earth showing the lines of latitude, including the Equator.

Equator (0°)

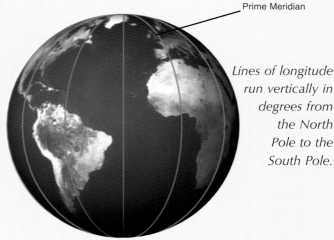

Prime Meridian

Lines of longitude run vertically in degrees from the North Pole to the South Pole.

LATITUDE

The most important line of latitude is the Equator, which is the imaginary line around the middle of the Earth. The other lines of latitude are measured in degrees north or south of the Equator. There are 90° either side of the Equator because this makes a half circle, which has 180° (think of the degrees on a protractor). Each line of latitude is about 111 km apart.

LONGITUDE

Lines of longitude are measured in degrees east or west of a line that goes from the North Pole to the South Pole through a place called Greenwich, in London, England. This line is called the Prime Meridian. The Prime Meridian, and the opposite 180th meridian (at 180° longitude) separate the eastern and western hemispheres. A specific longitude can be combined with a specific latitude to give a precise position on the Earth's surface.

TRAVEL THE WORLD

Using an atlas or an online map, find the latitude and longitude reference for the place you live in. Then choose five countries you have visited already or have always wanted to visit. See if you can find the latitude and longitude references for some of the cities or other places of interest in those countries. Make a chart or database showing your results.

Perhaps you could give a presentation about why you chose these places, explaining where they are in the world, what the climate and landscape is like and how the people live and work.

You might also want to find out how the time in your chosen places differs from the time where you live. The Earth spins round a full 360° every 24 hours, so every 15° of longitude equals about one hour of time on Earth (360 ÷ 24 = 15). By comparing the longitude of two places, you can roughly estimate how many hours earlier or later the time will be. Places to the west of your location will have an earlier time; places to the east will have a later time.

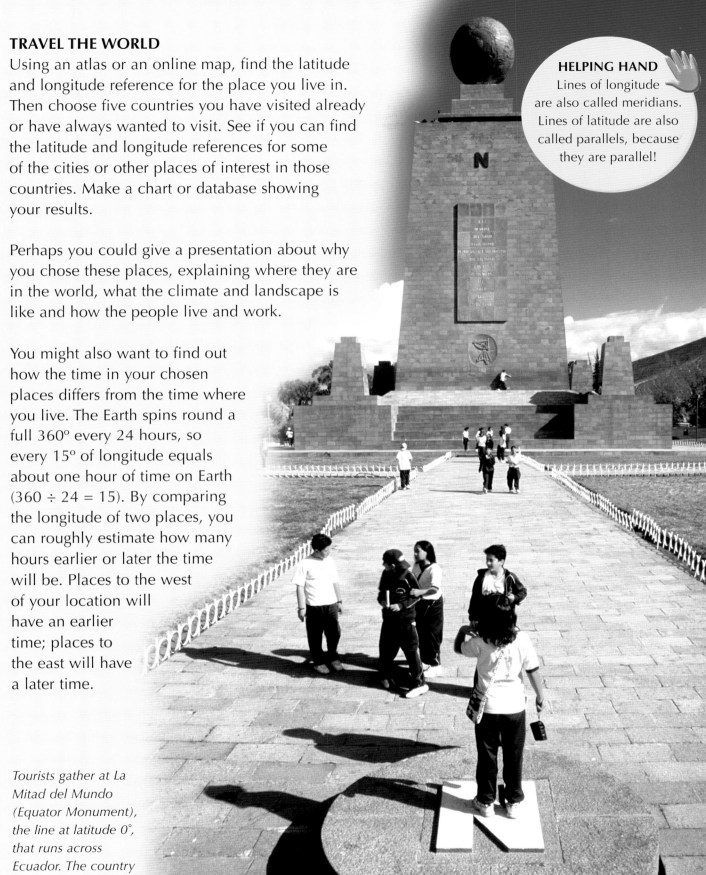

Tourists gather at La Mitad del Mundo (Equator Monument), the line at latitude 0°, that runs across Ecuador. The country is named after this famous line.

Explaining a round world

More than 2,000 years ago, Ancient Greek mathematicians guessed that the Earth was round. It was not until 500 years ago, however, that explorers sailed right round the world and proved that it really was shaped like a ball.

Photos taken from space clearly show the true shape of the Earth.

GLOBES

A round model of the Earth is called a globe. It is the only way to map the world accurately. You can spin a globe round to see the whole world. A globe shows the correct positions of the land and water on the surface of the Earth. It also shows how large they are in relation to each other. Water covers more than two-thirds of the Earth. Viewed from one side, a globe looks nearly all blue because of the vast area of the Pacific Ocean.

A globe can be rotated 360° to show the entire world.

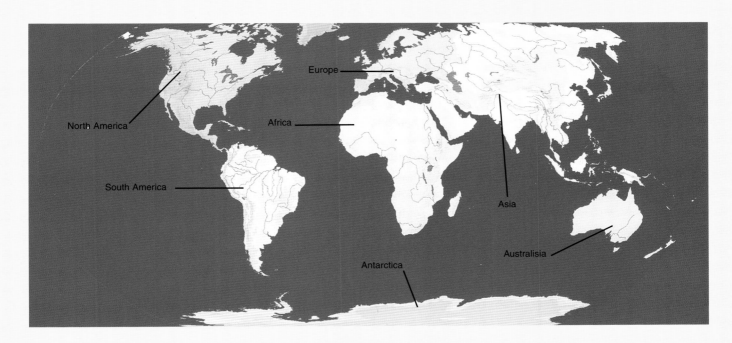

North America
Europe
Africa
South America
Asia
Australisia
Antarctica

CONTINENTS

The large areas of land on the Earth's surface are called continents. There are seven continents – Africa, Antarctica, Asia, Australia, Europe and North and South America.

GLOBES AND MAPS

Globes are not easy to carry around and you cannot fold them up and put them in your pocket, like a flat map. Try making a flat map of the world from a globe. Ask a friend to hold the globe still while you trace around the edges of the continents on a thin sheet of paper. Do not include too much detail; just trace a general outline shape for each continent.

Look back at the globe to position the continents roughly in the correct places in relation to each other. Label and colour each continent and the oceans between them. Do not forget to give your map a title and a date.

Compare your map and the globe with world maps in atlases (books of maps) or on the Internet. What differences can you see? Look carefully at the sizes of the different continents and their location in relation to each other. Which of the flat maps looksmost similar to the globe?

KEY SKILLS

 Drawing sketch maps

 Using online atlases

Analysing evidence and drawing conclusions; interpreting maps

HELPING HAND
Some useful websites for world maps are:
http://worldatlas.com/atlas/world.htm
http://www.nationalgeographic.com/maps/
http://www.gesource.ac.uk/worldguide/worldmap.html

Round Earth, flat maps

A flat map of a large area can never show the Earth's curved surface accurately. The shape or size of the continents and oceans has to be distorted to fit the flat surface. These flat maps are called projections. There are hundreds of different kinds of projections. Some are good for one job, but useless for another. Map makers have to choose the projection that best suits their purpose.

PROJECTION PROBLEMS

Most projections are worked out using mathematics. You can see how they work if you imagine shining a light through a glass globe so that the latitude and longitude lines are projected onto a flat sheet of paper. Members of a Polar Race team used a map like the one on the right, which is based on a Planar, or azimuthal projection, to find their way to the North Pole.

KEY SKILLS

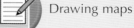
Drawing maps

Asking geographical questions

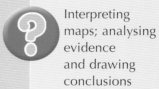
Interpreting maps; analysing evidence and drawing conclusions

A map showing the route taken around Canada to the North Pole by a Polar Race team.

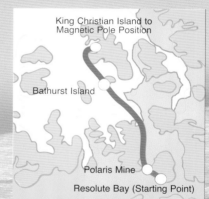

King Christian Island to Magnetic Pole Position

Bathurst Island

Polaris Mine

Resolute Bay (Starting Point)

These explorers use a conic projection to help them find their way to the North Pole.

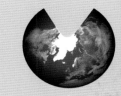

CYLINDRICAL PROJECTION

This is made as if a globe has been wrapped in a tube, or cylinder, of paper. Directions are accurate, but scale differs from one part of the map to another and land areas are badly distorted. Africa looks smaller than North America, when it is really 5,180,000 square kilometres larger. Australia also looks smaller than Greenland, when it is in fact three times larger. If the sizes are corrected, then the shapes are distorted instead.

CONIC PROJECTION

This type of projection is made as if a cone-shaped 'hat' of paper has been placed over a globe, touching it at one line of latitude. The fan-shaped map becomes less accurate, however, the further away you get from this line. A conic projection map is useful for mapping countries in the middle of the globe such as Russia or the United States.

PLANAR, OR AZIMUTHAL PROJECTION

This is made as if a flat sheet of paper touches the globe at one point in the middle of the map, such as the North or the South Pole. Further away from this point, the map becomes increasingly distorted.

HELPING HAND
The most important thing to remember about projections is that there will always be some error and distortion on a projected map.

WHICH PROJECTION?

Do some research on the Internet and in bookshops and libraries and see how many different projections you can find. Imagine you are running a map-making company, which makes maps for a variety of different clients. Which projections do you think would be most suitable for the following purposes?

- Explorers planning an expedition to the North Pole.
- A charity that works mainly with countries in the southern hemisphere (southern half of the world).
- A global shipping company that needs to give directions to its many shipping lines.
- A university geography department.

- A medical team flying into a disaster area to help injured people.
- Television staff working on a documentary about Greenland.
- Geographers mapping Brazil's population.

Produce a map for one of these clients, explaining why this is the best map for them.

Where in the world?

The Global Positioning System (GPS) is a system of satellites and radio receivers, which gives an accurate position of something almost anywhere in the world, in any weather, during the day or at night. GPS was developed by the United States Department of Defense, and its official name is NAVSTAR (Navigation Signal Timing and Ranging) GPS. It is an important tool in map making and is also used to help with navigation in cars, aeroplanes and ships.

KEY SKILLS

Presenting information and data

Interpreting maps

Organising geographic information

Carrying out field work

HOW GPS WORKS

The 24 satellites that are used for GPS travel round the Earth twice a day about 20,200 km above the surface. These satellites transmit radio signals, which will pass through clouds, glass and plastic but are blocked by solid objects, such as buildings. A GPS receiver picks up these radio signals and calculates how far away the satellites are. With the signals from four or more satellites, the receiver can work out the latitude, longitude and altitude of its position and the precise time. It can also calculate other data, such as speed and distance to destination.

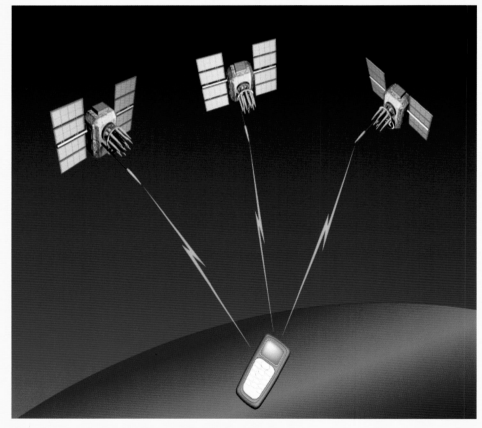

A network of satellites constantly circles the Earth, sending down information to GPS receivers.

BE A SURVEYOR

The idea of fixing the position of a point on the Earth's surface using measurements from several different locations has been used since the early days of map making. Surveyors would map a piece of land by dividing it into a network of triangles and recording the positions of the points at the corners of the triangles. This method is called triangulation. You can try this yourself.

Choose a small area and measure a short distance between two points. This is your base line. Standing at one end of the base line, measure the angle to a feature in the distance, such as a tree or a gate. You can use a protractor or a theodolite to measure the angle. Then go to the other end of the line and measure the angle to the same point.

This GPS receiver is being used by a firefighter to work out the fastest route to an emergency. The display shows the fire-engine's position as it drives towards its destination.

The three points form a triangle. As the three angles in a triangle add up to 180°, you can work out the third angle without measuring it. From the length of the base line and all three angles, you can also work out the length of the other two sides of the triangle mathematically. This gives you the distance to the feature from both ends of the base line without having to measure it. Repeat the same method for other features and record your triangles on a scale plan of the area.

HELPING HAND
Look at
http://earth.google.com
to zoom in on satellite photos
of specific locations around
the world.

Glossary

Altitude
The height of something, usually measured as a distance above sea level or above the Earth's surface.

Bearing
The position of a place or object in relation to another.

Carbon dioxide
A gas found in the air. It is one of the biggest contributers to global warming.

Choropleth map
A map that uses shades or colours to show information about regions within an area.

Climate
The average weather conditions of a certain area.

Cold front
The boundary in the atmosphere where an advancing mass of cold air pushes at a mass of warmer air.

Contour line
A line on a map that connects points of equal height.

Data
A collection of facts from which conclusions may be drawn.

Flow line map
A map that uses lines and arrows to show information about a place or places.

GIS (Geographical Information System)
A computer system that brings together all types of information about a place.

GPS (Global Positioning System)
A radio-navigation system that allows people to find out their exact location anywhere in the world, at any time and in any weather conditions.

Global warming
A gradual increase in the average temperature of the Earth's atmosphere.

Grid reference
A point on a map, defined by two sets of numbers or letters – the first set corresponds to a vertical gridline and the second to a horizontal one.

Hachures
Short lines used on maps to show slopes and their steepness and direction.

Isoline
A line on a map connecting points of equal value.

Key/legend
A list that explains what symbols, colours and abbreviations on a map mean.

Line of latitude
Also called a parallel. An imaginary circle around Earth, running from east to west, parallel to the Equator.

Line of longitude
Also called a meridian. An imaginary circle around Earth, passing through the North and South Poles, at right angles to the Equator.

Magnetic north
The direction towards which a compass arrow points. Magnetic north differs from True North because Earth's magnetic fields are not directly in line with the North and South Poles.

Prime Meridian
The line of 0° longitude that passes from the North Pole to the South Pole through Greenwich, England.

Projection
The representation of a three-dimensional object, such as the globe, on a flat surface, such as a map.

Raster data
A digital method of storing information using cells, or pixels, arranged in a regular grid pattern.

Relief map
A map that shows the shape of the land in three-dimensions.

Scale
A system of numbering used on maps where one unit on the map represents a number of the same units on the ground.

Spot height
A position on a map where the exact height of land is known and marked.

Stevenson screen
A white, ventilated box that contains weather instruments, such as thermometers and barometers, for measuring current weather conditions.

Surveyor
A specialist who measures, maps and collects land data about land and its features.

Synoptic chart
A map showing weather conditions over a large area at a given time.

Topological map
A simplified map where unnecessary detail has been removed to make the relevant information clear.

True North
The position of the North Pole.

Vector data
A digital method of storing information using coordinates (X,Y) to represent locations on Earth.

Warm front
The boundary where an advancing mass of warm air pushes at a mass of cooler air.

Weblinks

http://www.multimap.com
Online maps of every country in the world. Click on different locations to zoom in.

http://www.bbc.co.uk/schools/gcsebitesize/geography/geogskills/geogskillsmapsrev1.shtml
Revision-based website from the BBC. This section focuses on basic map skills.

http://www.metoffice.gov.uk/
Website of the Meteorlogical (Met) Office featuring weather maps and pressure charts.

http://www.ordnancesurvey.co.uk/oswebsite/
Website of Ordnance Survey – the national mapping agency of Great Britain. The site includes access to the "Free Maps" initiative.

http://www.nla.gov.au/map/cartolinks.html
This website from the National Library of Australia features a wide range of links to historical, aerial, weather and road maps.

http://www.gis.com/
The online guide to Geographical Information Systems.

http://nationalmap.gov/
Website of the US Geological Survey featuring "The National Map", a highly detailed "clickable" map of the USA.

http://wwp.greenwichmeridian.com/
Maps, information and links from the home of the Prime Meridian in Greenwich, England.

Note to parents and teachers:

Every effort has been made by the Publishers to ensure that these websites are suitable for children, that they are of the highest educational value, and that they contain no inappropriate or offensive material. However, because of the nature of the Internet, it is impossible to guarantee that the contents of these sites will not be altered. We strongly advise that Internet access is supervised by a responsible adult.

Index